Greece

ANCIENT CIVILIZATIONS

Greg Banks

PICTURE CREDITS

Cover: Parthenon, Greece © Werner Forman/Corbis/Tranz.

Page 1 © The Granger Collection, New York; page 4 (left) © Fine Art Photographic Library/Corbis/Tranz; page 4 (right) © Historical Picture Archive/Corbis/Tranz; page 5 (top) © moreimages.com; page 5 (bottom left) © Fine Art Photographic Library/Corbis/Tranz; page 5 (bottom right) © Stapleton Collection/Corbis/Tranz; page 6 © Wolfgang Kaehler/Corbis/Tranz; page 9 © Gail Mooney/Corbis/Tranz; pages 12–15 © The Granger Collection, New York; page 16 (top) © Gianni Dagli Orti/Corbis/Tranz; page 16 (middle) © Dave G. Houser/Post-Houserstock/Corbis/Tranz; page 16 (bottom) © Araldo de Luca/Corbis/Tranz; page 18 © Vanni Archive/Corbis/Tranz; page 21 © Werner Forman/Corbis/Tranz; page 22 (top) © Todd Gipstein/Corbis/Tranz; page 22 (bottom) © Wolfgang Kaehler/Corbis/Tranz; page 23 © North Wind Picture Archives; page 24 © Bettmann/Corbis/Tranz; page 25 © The Granger Collection, New York; page 26 © Rainer Hackenberg/Corbis/Tranz; page 29, Digital Vision.

Produced through the worldwide resources of the National Geographic Society, John M. Fahey, Jr., President and Chief Executive Officer; Gilbert M. Grosvenor, Chairman of the Board.

PREPARED BY NATIONAL GEOGRAPHIC SCHOOL PUBLISHING
Sheron Long, Chief Executive Officer; Samuel Gesumaria, President; Steve Mico, Executive Vice President and Publisher; Francis Downey, Editor in Chief; Richard Easby, Editorial Manager; Margaret Sidlosky, Director of Design and Illustrations; Jim Hiscott, Design Manager; Cynthia Olson and Ruth Ann Thompson, Art Directors; Matt Wascavage, Director of Publishing Services; Lisa Pergolizzi, Production Manager.

MANUFACTURING AND QUALITY CONTROL
Christopher A. Liedel, Chief Financial Officer; Phillip L. Schlosser, Vice President; Clifton M. Brown III, Director.

EDITOR
Mary Anne Wengel

PROGRAM CONSULTANTS
Dr. Shirley V. Dickson, National Literacy Consultant; Margit E. McGuire, Ph.D., Professor of Teacher Education and Social Studies, Seattle University.

National Geographic Theme Sets program developed by Macmillan Education Australia Pty Limited.

Copyright © 2007 National Geographic Society.
All rights reserved. Reproduction of the whole or any part of the contents without written permission from the publisher is prohibited. National Geographic, National Geographic School Publishing, and the Yellow Border are registered trademarks of the National Geographic Society.

Published by the National Geographic Society
1145 17th Street, N.W.
Washington, D.C. 20036-4688

ISBN: 978-1-4263-5162-4

Product# 4P1005169

Printed in Hong Kong.

2011 2010 2009 2008 2007
2 3 4 5 6 7 8 9 10 11 12 13 14 15

Contents

- Ancient Civilizations 4
- Ancient Greece 6
- Think About the Key Concepts 17

Visual Literacy
Timeline 18

Genre Study
Informational Report 20

Greek Temples 21

- Apply the Key Concepts 27

Research and Write
Create Your Own Report 28

Glossary 31

Index 32

Ancient Civilizations

A civilization grows when people settle in a place and, over time, develop a society. It has a written language, a form of government, a set of beliefs, and a common culture. Egypt, China, Greece, and Rome are four ancient civilizations. Their history still fascinates people today.

Key Concepts

1. Ancient civilizations were shaped by their locations.
2. Ancient civilizations were complex societies.
3. Ancient civilizations produced lasting achievements.

Four Ancient Civilizations

Egypt

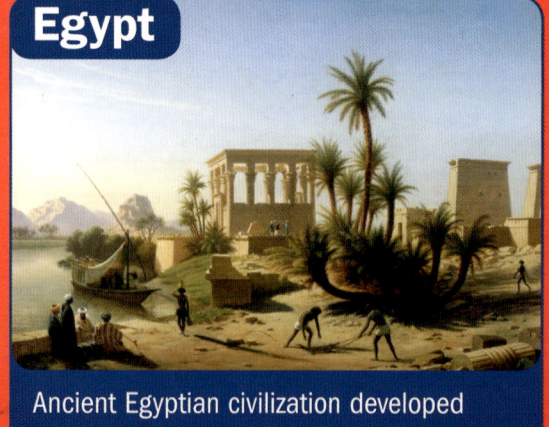

Ancient Egyptian civilization developed along the banks of the Nile River.

China

Ancient Chinese civilization developed on the banks of the Huang and Yangtze Rivers.

In this book you will learn about the lives of ancient Greek people.

Greece

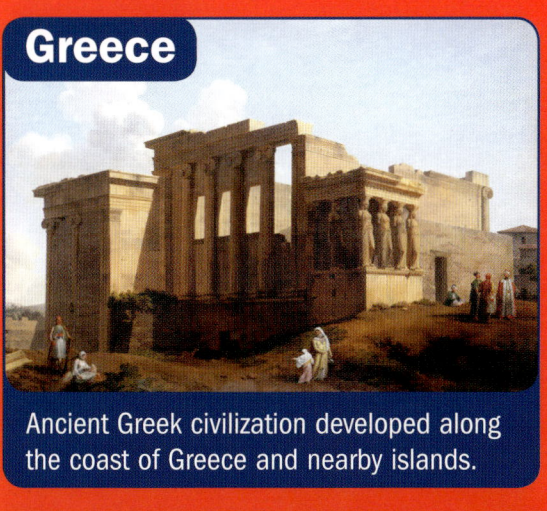

Ancient Greek civilization developed along the coast of Greece and nearby islands.

Rome

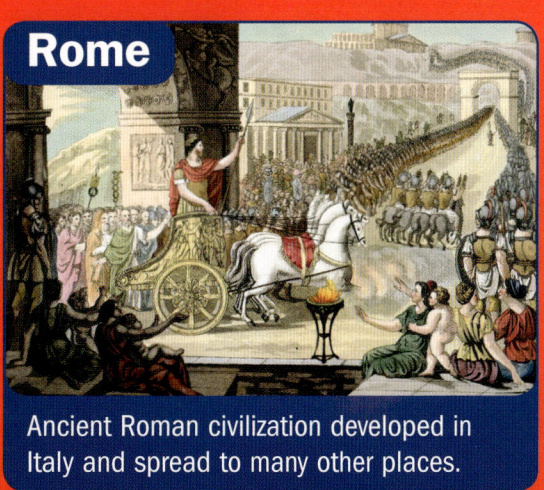

Ancient Roman civilization developed in Italy and spread to many other places.

Ancient Greece

Imagine taking a walk around the streets of a city in ancient Greece. You might see many houses made of mud bricks with tile roofs. You might see beautiful temples built with rows of huge stone columns. You might see the temples of the Acropolis rising over the city in the distance. What do you think life would have been like in ancient Greece? Read on to find out.

Greece Today

Greece is a country in Europe. Africa lies to the south of Greece, and Asia lies to the east. Greece has a rocky mainland and 1,500 islands. The islands are scattered in the Ionian and Aegean Seas. The Greek mainland is a **peninsula.** The jagged coastline is surrounded on three sides by water.

A temple called the Parthenon rises high over the Greek city of Athens.

Albania, Macedonia, and Bulgaria are countries to the north of Greece. The country of Turkey is to the east.

The yellow area on the map below shows Greece as it is today.

Map of Greece

Key Concept 1 Ancient civilizations were shaped by their locations.

Where People Settled

Ancient Greeks settled in **locations** along the coast. Greece has many mountains and little flat land. In places, the coast is rocky. It rises straight up from the water below. The rugged terrain of the mainland and the islands led the people of ancient Greece to settle along the coast.

locations
places or sites

The earliest Greeks were called the Minoans. They settled on the large island of Crete. Crete is south of the mainland. The Minoans settled here some time before 2600 B.C. Later, people called the Mycenaeans settled the southern tip of the mainland.

Map of Ancient Greece

Why People Settled

Ancient Greeks settled near the ocean. The ocean was a source of food and a means of travel. High mountains made it difficult to travel across the land. It was easier to travel around the coast by boat. The ancient Greeks became good sailors. They sailed between Crete and the mainland to trade.

Greece has a **temperate** climate. A temperate climate is good for growing crops and raising animals. However, the land in Greece is not very **fertile.** Most of it is rocky and not good for farming. The Minoans grew wheat in the most fertile areas on Crete. They grew olives and grapes in the poorer soil.

This Minoan ruin at Knossos on Crete looks out over farmland.

The Minoans built cities on Crete and other islands. They developed a written language. They used the language to keep records of trade. Around 1500 B.C., a volcano erupted and destroyed some of the Minoan cities. Later, in 1450 B.C., the Minoans were invaded by people from the Greek mainland. The Minoan civilization declined.

On the mainland, the Mycenaeans farmed, fished, and grew olives. Like the Minoans, they developed a written language and built cities. The Mycenaeans were good sailors. They traded goods, such as pottery and olive oil, around the Mediterranean Sea.

Around 1150 B.C., people called the Dorians invaded the Greek mainland from the north. The Dorians discovered how to make things out of iron. The ancient Greeks learned to smelt iron ore. They used the iron to make tools and weapons. This time period was known as the Iron Age.

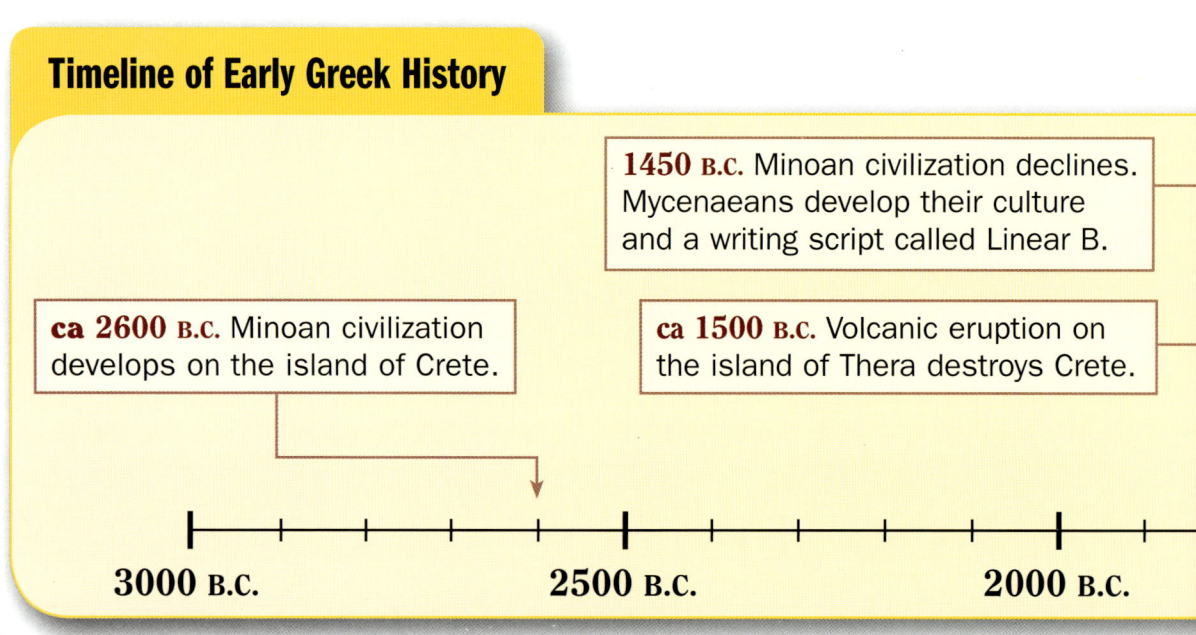

Timeline of Early Greek History

ca 2600 B.C. Minoan civilization develops on the island of Crete.

1450 B.C. Minoan civilization declines. Mycenaeans develop their culture and a writing script called Linear B.

ca 1500 B.C. Volcanic eruption on the island of Thera destroys Crete.

3000 B.C.   2500 B.C.   2000 B.C.

Becoming a Civilization

The different cultures of the Minoans, the Mycenaeans, and the Dorians influenced the way ancient Greece developed as a **civilization.** They each contributed to the culture of Greece.

civilization
a large society of people with a common culture

The ancient Greeks traded with one another. In time, the bigger Greek towns became cities. These cities did not join together to form one nation. Instead, the cities became independent **city-states.** The Greek word for a city-state was *polis*. A polis included a city and the villages and farmland that surrounded it. The most well-known city-states were Corinth, Olympia, Athens, and Sparta.

Each city-state had its own customs, religion, and **dialect.** Each city-state also had its own ruler. The rulers only united with neighboring city-states in times of war.

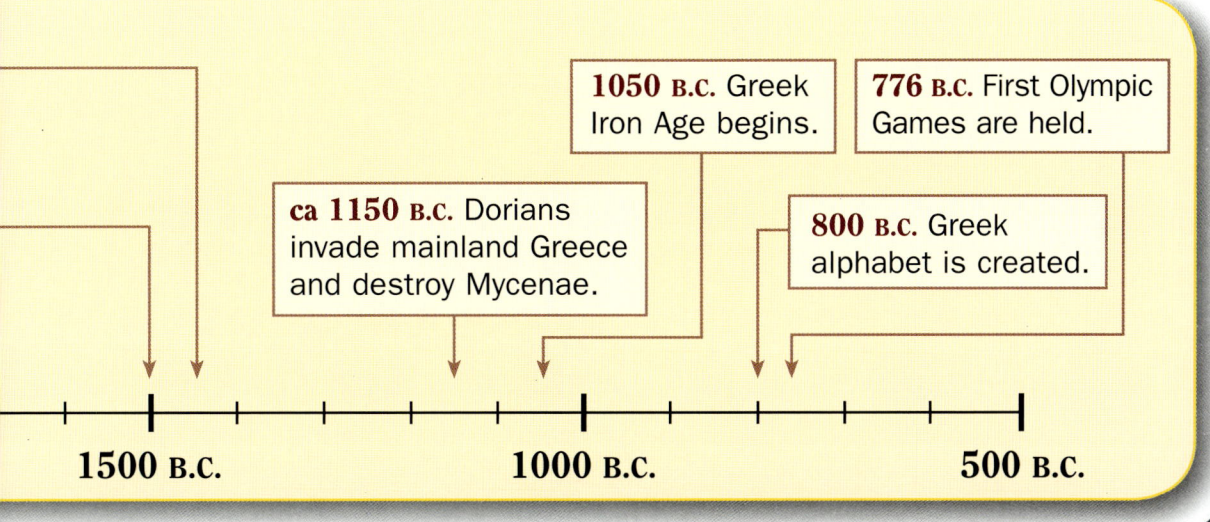

 **Key Concept 2** Ancient civilizations were complex societies.

Daily Life in Ancient Greece

Daily life was similar in all Greek city-states, except Sparta. Sparta was a **military state.** This meant that everyone's life revolved around the army. Most Spartan men were soldiers. Boys were sent to military school when they were six or seven. Here they learned to be soldiers. Girls had military training too.

In all other city-states, such as Athens, people were mainly farmers or traders. The rich people lived in big houses that opened onto a courtyard. They often kept slaves. Slaves farmed or worked in their businesses. Other people lived in small houses made of mud bricks with tile roofs.

Men mainly worked outside the home. Women stayed home and took care of the house and family. In Athens, all boys went to school. Boys from rich families had more schooling than boys from poor families. They learned how to read and write. Girls did not go to school. They learned household skills from their mothers.

These Greek women are working in the home.

Government

The city-states developed their own form of government. In early Mycenae, kings who made their own laws ruled city-states. Eventually, only a few city-states, such as Sparta, still had kings. Small groups of rich men governed most city-states.

In time, many city-states, such as Athens, started a new form of government. This new form of government was called a **democracy.** In a democracy, many people can have a say in what the government does.

All male **citizens** could vote in an assembly that governed Athens. They made decisions by **voting.** A council ran everyday matters of government for the assembly. Each year, citizens drew lots to choose 500 men to serve on the council. Men could not serve on the council for more than two years. Women, slaves, and foreigners were not allowed to vote.

Sparta was not as democratic as Athens. Two kings were leaders of the army. Not many people were citizens in Sparta. Not many people in Sparta were allowed to vote.

Pericles was a famous Athenian who supported democracy.

Beliefs

Ancient Greeks believed in and worshipped many gods and goddesses. They believed that the gods and goddesses lived together as a family on Mount Olympus. Zeus, the sky god, was the father and head of the family. Zeus's wife, Hera, was the goddess of women. Zeus and Hera had many children. Each one represented parts of Greek life. For example, one son, Apollo, was the god of healing. He was also the god of the sun.

Each city-state had its own special gods. Ancient Greeks built temples where people went to worship. One of the most important temples was the temple of Apollo at Delphi. Ancient Greeks came to Delphi to talk to their gods. They talked to their gods through a priest or priestess called an **oracle.** If a person wanted to ask a god a question, they would go to an oracle. The oracle would ask the god the question, then give the person the god's advice.

There are many stories about Zeus in Greek mythology.

Key Concept 3 Ancient civilizations produced lasting achievements.

Achievements of Ancient Greece

Ancient Greek history is full of lasting **achievements.** Many of these achievements influence our lives today. Many words in the English language come from Greek words. Greeks developed concepts that are still used in mathematics and science today. Greeks discovered that Earth is round and travels around the sun. People today still use ideas Greeks had about building and art.

achievements
things finished successfully with effort

Pythagoras was an important Greek mathematican. He is best remembered for the Pythagorean Theorem. If you know the lengths of two sides of a right triangle, you can use the Pythagorean Theorem to find the length of the third side of the triangle.

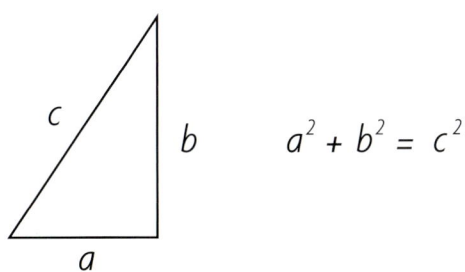

$a^2 + b^2 = c^2$

The Pythagorean Theorem

Pythagoras is known as "the father of numbers."

The ancient Greeks developed new ways of building. They found ways of making stone columns. The columns were built in a row called a colonnade. All of the columns were fluted. This means they had long rounded grooves. Many were carved at the top. The best-known columns are called Doric columns. They are named for the Dorians who first used them. These same kinds of columns are used in buildings today.

Columns at the ancient Greek temple of Hephaistion

Ancient Greeks made and decorated pots. They made pots out of clay and a metal called bronze. They often painted the pots with pictures of their gods. They also painted other things that were important, such as athletes at the Olympic Games. The art on these pots helps us learn more about how the ancient Greeks lived.

Columns at the modern Philadelphia Museum of Art

Greeks stored wine, oils, olives, and fish in pots such this one.

Think About the Key Concepts

Think about what you read. Think about the pictures and diagrams. Use these to answer the questions. Share what you think with others.

1. Where did people choose to settle? Why did they choose these locations?

2. How did the ancient civilization in this book develop over time?

3. What did members of a family living in this ancient civilization do each day?

4. What kind of government did the ancient civilization in this book have?

Visual Literacy: Timeline

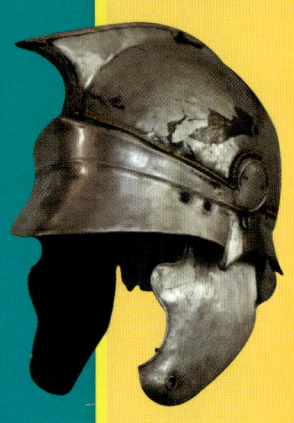

Ancient Greek helmet

A timeline shows the order in which important past events happened.

A timeline is a line with dates marked on it. Each important event or period is described in a box above or below the timeline. A line or arrow links each box to the date when the event happened.

Timelines can show different things.

Look at the timeline on pages 10–11. It shows events in ancient Greek history. The timeline on pages 18–19 shows important Greek wars.

Wars and Politics of Ancient Greece

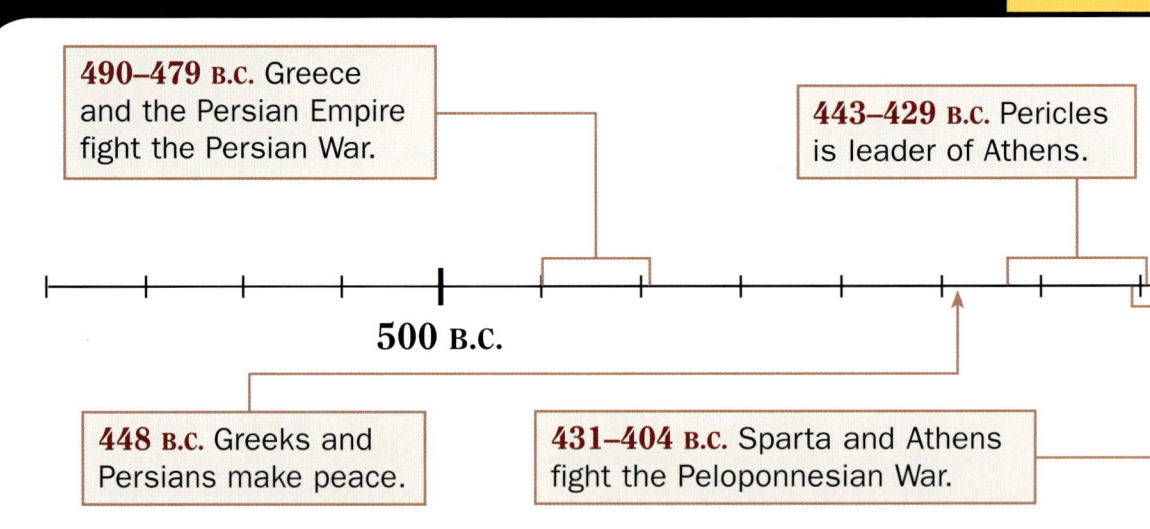

490–479 B.C. Greece and the Persian Empire fight the Persian War.

443–429 B.C. Pericles is leader of Athens.

500 B.C.

448 B.C. Greeks and Persians make peace.

431–404 B.C. Sparta and Athens fight the Peloponnesian War.

How to Read a Timeline

1. Read the title.
The title tells you the subject of the timeline.

2. Read the labels.
Read the label at the start of the timeline first. Then read across to the end of the timeline.

3. Look at the dates.
Follow the lines that link the labels to the years marked on the timeline.

4. Think about what you learned.
Think about how the timeline helps you learn the history of the topic.

What Did You Learn?

Read the timeline by following the steps above. What have you learned from the timeline? What do you now know about the wars the ancient Greeks fought? Share what you learned with a classmate.

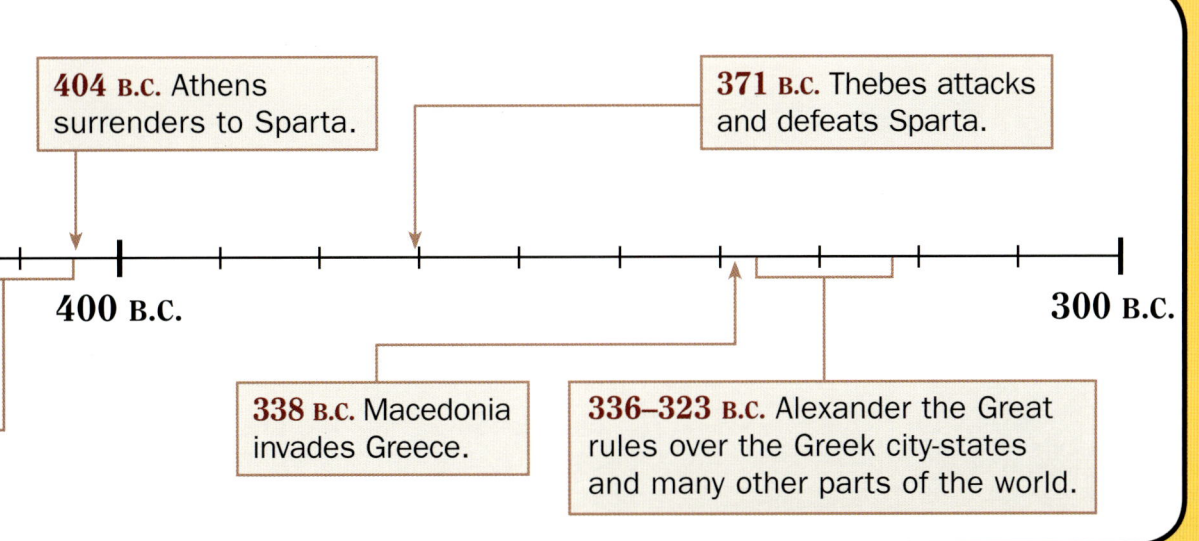

404 B.C. Athens surrenders to Sparta.

371 B.C. Thebes attacks and defeats Sparta.

338 B.C. Macedonia invades Greece.

336–323 B.C. Alexander the Great rules over the Greek city-states and many other parts of the world.

400 B.C. — 300 B.C.

GENRE STUDY

Informational Report

An **informational report** gives important information about a topic. The report starting on page 21 gives historical information about Greek temples.

An informational report includes the following:

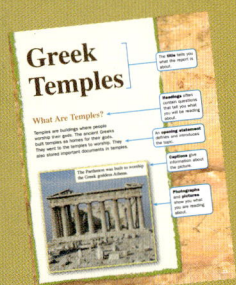

The **title** tells you what the report is about.

Headings contain questions that tell you what you will be reading about.

The **opening statement** defines and introduces the topic.

Text answers the questions in the headings.

Photographs and **pictures** show you what you are reading about.

The **conclusion** signals the end of the report. It may summarize the article or make a closing remark.

Greek Temples

The **title** tells you what the report is about.

What Are Temples?

Headings often contain questions that tell you what you will be reading about.

Temples are buildings where people worship their gods. The ancient Greeks built temples as homes for their gods. They went to the temples to worship. They also stored important documents in temples.

An **opening statement** defines and introduces the topic.

Captions give information about the picture.

The Parthenon was built to worship the Greek goddess Athena.

Photographs and **pictures** show you what you are reading about.

What Did Greek Temples Look Like?

Some people think that the first Greek temples were built to look like large Greek homes. Early temples had one big room. These early temples were made of wood or mud bricks. Roofs were made of straw.

Later, temples were built from stone, such as limestone and marble. Roofs were made of terra-cotta tiles. The temple base was made of stone slabs. It was either a square or a rectangle. Three stone steps led up to an inside room. A row of columns, called a colonnade, ran along the top of these steps. Some Greek temples had a colonnade only at the front. The inside room, called a *cella*, was square. Another row of columns on two, or all four, sides often lined the *cella*.

Text answers the questions in the headings.

Terra-cotta tiles on a roof

This Greek temple has a six-columned colonnade.

There was only one door into the *cella*. This door let in light when it was open. Inside the *cella* was a statue of the god or goddess the temple was dedicated to.

The Greeks used many simple tools to build their temples. They used wooden pins to help them split rock. They drove rows of pins into the rock. Then they wet the pins so that the wood would expand. When the wooden pins expanded, the rock split. Rocks were put onto two-wheeled carts. Donkeys pulled the carts to the building site.

The Greeks used a type of hammer and chisel to shape the stone blocks and to carve statues of their gods. Workers used simple cranes fitted with pulleys and rope to lift the large stone blocks.

This statue of Athena stood inside the *cella* at the Parthenon in Athens.

Who Built Temples?

People in Greek villages first built simple temples. As the villages grew into cities, the Greeks built more and bigger temples. Many more people were needed to build these large temples.

In time, the government of a city or a rich citizen would hire an architect to build a temple. The architect planned the temple, hired people to do the work, and made sure the work got done.

Building a large temple in ancient Greece involved many people.

Why Were Temples Built?

Greek temples were built as homes for Greek gods. They were also used to store records and other documents.

The Greeks believed that their gods watched over people and protected them. That is why they built temples. Greeks came to the temple to bring offerings to the gods. They brought food, gold, and silver. The Greeks also held religious processions and festivals on the grounds around the temples. Animals may have been sacrificed at these festivals.

Greeks went to special temples to ask their gods for advice. A priest or priestess, called an oracle, spoke to the gods and told people what the gods said in reply.

When Were Temples Built?

The first Greek temples were built in the Archaic Period, which was between 750 B.C. and 500 B.C. People who study history think that ancient Greeks may have built temples even before that time. These would have been built with mud and wood. No examples of these earlier temples have survived to the present day.

During the Classical Period, from 500 B.C. to 336 B.C., people built many temples. Fewer temples were built after this time.

The Greeks believed that oracles could communicate with gods.

Where Were Temples Built?

Temples were usually built on hills above cities where they could be easily protected from attackers. The Greeks often built rock walls around a temple. This area was called an acropolis. The acropolis became the religious and military center of the city.

Why Are Temples Important?

People from all over Greece visited temples. They came to worship and get advice. Today, the ancient Greek temples are in ruins. People admire the ruined temples. The ruins attract many tourists. The temples help people appreciate the achievements of the ancient Greeks.

> A **conclusion** may summarize the report or make a closing remark.

The ruins of the Tholos Temple at Delphi

Apply the Key Concepts

Key Concept 1 Ancient civilizations were shaped by their locations.

Activity The geography of Greece affected where its civilization developed. Create a two-column chart. List the geographical features of Greece in the first column. List the effect each feature had on the development of the civilization in the second column.

Geographical Features	Effects

Key Concept 2 Ancient civilizations were complex societies.

Activity Imagine you live in ancient Greece. What is your job? What do you wear? What do you eat? What do you believe in? Write a short essay about your life and what you do each day.

I am a Greek philosopher . . .

Key Concept 3 Ancient civilizations produced lasting achievements.

Activity Some of the art and buildings of ancient Greece still exist today. Find a picture of something created in ancient Greece. Write down what you like or find interesting about the picture.

I like Greek pots because . . .

Create Your Own Report

An informational report is a short report that gives people information about a topic.

1. Study the Model

Look back at the description of an informational report on page 20. Then read the informational report on pages 21–26 again. Note how the report is organized. Can you see how the headings help organize the information? What details did the writer include to make the text informative? In what ways did these details add interest to the topic?

Writing an Informational Report
- Write an opening statement that defines and introduces the topic.
- Use headings to organize the information.
- Questions often make good headings.
- Use pictures to add interest.
- Write a conclusion.

2. Choose Your Topic

Get together with a few other students in a small group. Choose a general topic in history that you are all interested in. Divide the topic up. For example, the topic "Greek gods" can be divided up into smaller topics, such as "What legends are there about Greek gods?" and "How did Greeks worship their gods?" Have each person choose a part of the topic he or she is interested in. You are now ready to research and write an informational report together.

3. Research Your Topic

Ask yourself what you already know about this topic. Do you know enough to write an informational report? Make a list of questions that you will want to answer in your report. Remember to focus on useful information. Think about what your reader might like or need to know. Now go to the library or on the Internet to get answers to your questions.

> My Topic: Greek gods
> 1. What did the gods do?
> 2. Are there legends and stories about gods?
> 3. How did Greeks worship their gods?

4. Take Notes

Take notes of what you learn. As you gather new information, you may find that it leads to another question. Write the new questions down so that you do not forget them.

5. Write a Draft

Gather all the information you and your classmates have found. Does the information answer the questions you started with? Do you need to include new questions? Start writing a draft of the report, putting the questions and answers in an order that makes sense. If you need to, review the features of an informational report on page 20.

6. Revise and Edit

Reread your draft. Have you kept the information brief and to the point?

Create a Display of Reports

Follow the steps below to turn your draft into a report. Then you can share your work with your classmates.

Make and Share Your Report

1. Arrange the text.
Create the front page of your report. Put the title information on the front page. Arrange the rest of the text on the following pages. Each page should have a question followed by information that answers the question.

2. Include visuals.
Include visuals such as photographs or pictures to help clarify the information and add interest. Write captions and labels to help readers understand the visuals.

3. Create a display.
When every group's report is done, lay them all out on a table where others can read them.

4. Share and read.
Choose a report other than the one you wrote. Read it to learn more about the topic.

Glossary

achievements – things finished successfully with effort

ca – (short for "circa") a word used to show that a date is not known for sure

citizens – members of a city, state, or country who have certain rights and duties

city-states – regions or areas controlled by a city

civilization – a large society of people with a common culture

democracy – the ruling of a country by leaders elected by the people of that country

dialect – a regional way of speaking a language, including different ways of saying some words or using some different words

fertile – rich and good for growing crops

locations – places or sites

military state – a state in which people are trained to fight wars

oracle – a person who is believed to be able to consult with gods and goddesses

peninsula – a long, narrow piece of land that is surrounded by water on three sides

temperate – the type of weather found in places that are warm in summer and cold in winter

voting – the means by which people show their preferences

Index

Athens 8, 11–13

city-state 11–14

civilization 4–5, 11

columns 6, 16

Crete 8, 10

democracy 13

Dorians 10–11, 16

government 4, 13

Iron Age 10–11

mathematics 15

Minoans 8–11

Mycenaeans 8, 10–11

Olympic Games 11, 16

Pythagoras 15

slaves 12–13

Sparta 8, 11–13

temple 6, 14, 16